SHENANDOAH
National Park
by Ruth Radlauer

Photographs by
Ed and Ruth Radlauer

Design and map by
Rolf Zillmer

AN ELK GROVE BOOK

CHILDRENS PRESS, CHICAGO

With warm and special thanks to
Dennis Carter, Chief Naturalist,
and his fine staff

Photo credits:
    National Park Service Photos, pages 29 (snake),
      33 (fawn), 35 (bear), and 43
    Rolf Zillmer, cover and page 29 (poison ivy)

Cover: Fall Colors—Shenandoah

Library of Congress Cataloging in Publication Data

Radlauer, Ruth Shaw.
  Shenandoah National Park.
  (Parks for people)
  "An Elk Grove book."
  1. Shenandoah National Park (Va.)—Juvenile
literature. I. Radlauer, Ed. II. Zillmer,
Rolf. III. Title. IV. Series.
F232.S48R32   917.55'90443   81-15521
ISBN 0-516-07744-9   AACR2

Copyright © 1982 by Regensteiner Publishing Enterprises, Inc.
All rights reserved. Published simultaneously in Canada.
Printed in the United States of America.

2 3 4 5 6 7 8 9 10 11 12 13 14 15 R 88 87 86 85 84 83

Contents

	page
What is Shenandoah National Park?	4
Your Trip to Shenandoah	6
Map	7
Trail Talk	8
To Know a Mountain	10
Earth Story I	12
Earth Story II	14
Plant Parade—Succession	16
Flowers	18
Trees	20
And More Trees	22
Early Days	24
"Recycled" Park	26
Plan to be Safe	28
Furry Friends	30
Deer, Oh Deer	32
Bear Country	34
Big Meadow	36
A Guide to Forever?	38
Wilderness Ways	40
Winter	42
A Changing World	44
Other National Park Service Areas in the East	46
Author and Illustrators	48

What is Shenandoah National Park?

Shenandoah National Park is a place of change and color. The shape of the land changed many times before human eyes ever saw it. In the last 11,000 years, these mountains have changed from Indian hunting grounds to farmlands, and then to a national park.

Even today, Shenandoah changes from morning to night, season to season, and year to year. Each hour, each minute, the colors change. During winter and early spring, the hills look like gray velvet as millions of leafless trees stand and wait. Bright-colored flowers bask in warm sun before the trees "wake up" and spread their light green leaves.

Summer's green is darker. Later, autumn chills make the leaves fade, splashing mountains and hollows with fiery red and gold.

Shenandoah is trees and butterflies. It's the twinkle of black eyes peeking out of a burrow when you walk in the Big Meadow. It's brisk breezes at the top of Hawksbill and the tingly song your feet sing at the end of a long, hard hike.

In Shenandoah, it rains, it blows, fog drifts, the sun shines. Yes, every minute is different.

Fog Drifts

Spicebush Swallowtail Butterfly

Black Eyes Twinkle—Woodchuck

Ant, Acorn, Common Cinquefoil

Your Trip to Shenandoah

Even you will change while you visit Virginia's Shenandoah National Park. You need several days just to begin to know this place. To plan your park visit, write for an activity schedule and map and request a list of books you can buy. Or talk with a ranger as soon as you enter the park.

Shenandoah has 400 miles of foot trails and 150 miles of horse trails. Hikes can be long, short, up, down, or in a circuit. You'll want good hiking shoes or boots, a canteen, and rain gear. Layers of clothes help you keep warm, and you can peel off layers as the sun gets hot. A day pack leaves your hands free to balance or climb.

Several roads lead to four entrances to the park. You can get to Front Royal, Virginia, and the North Entrance by way of Highways I 66 and 340. From Washington, D.C., Highway I 66 and Highways 29 and 211 lead to Thornton Gap Entrance. Swift Run Gap Entrance is reached by Highway 33. Highway I 64 or the Blue Ridge Parkway takes you to the South Entrance. For information about lodges and campgrounds, write the Superintendent, Shenandoah National Park, Luray, Virginia 22835.

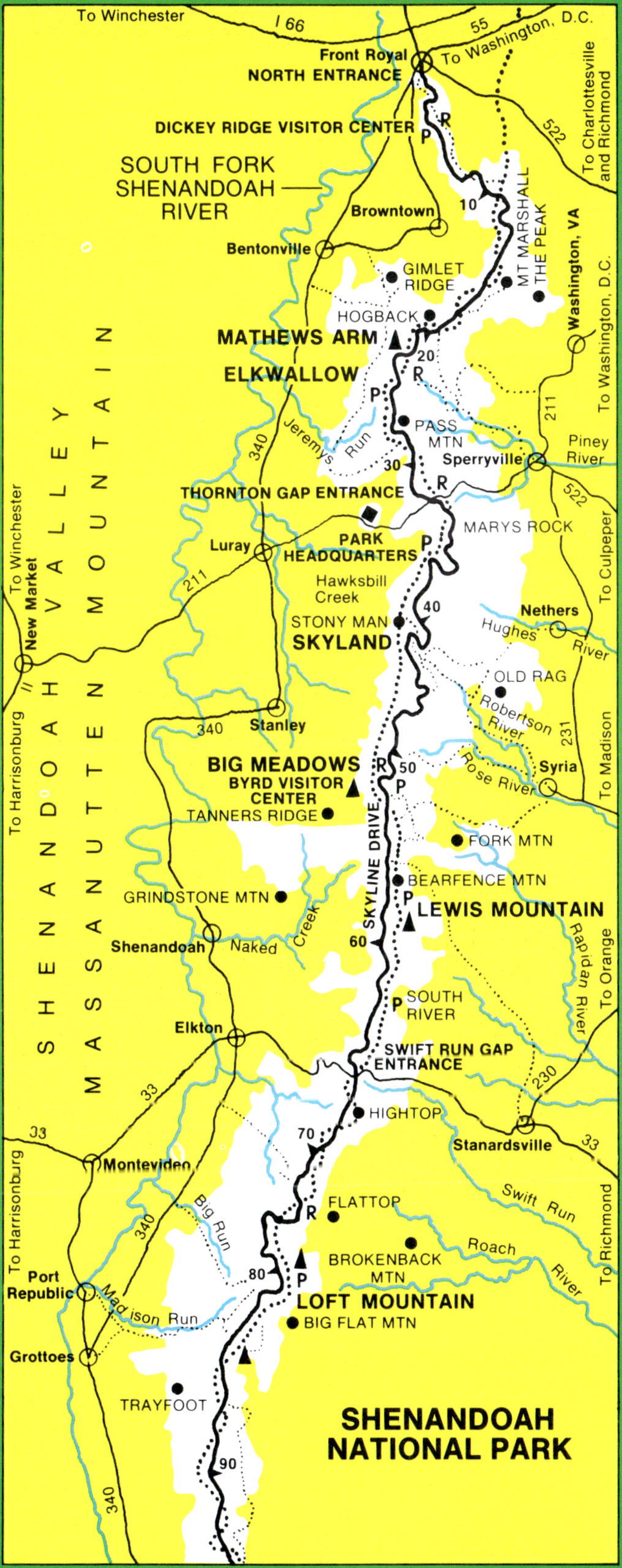

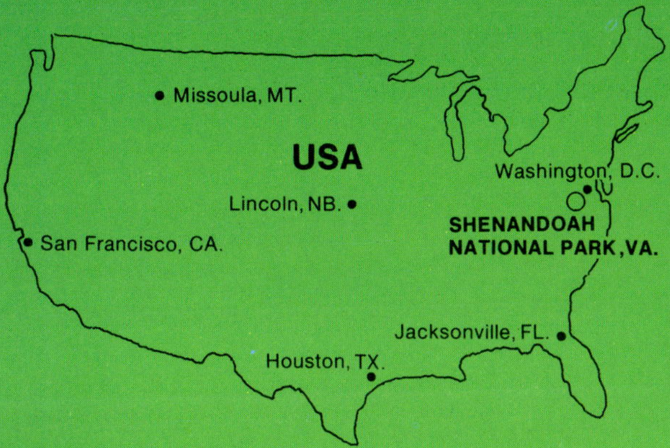

Campground ▲
Ranger Station R
Cabin, Building ■
Picnic Area P
Skyline Drive
Mileage Mark
Other Road
Appalachian Trail
Other Trail
Mountain ●

Miles 0 2 4 6.2
Kilometers 0 5 10

Trail Talk

It always helps to know the language. At Shenandoah, you'll hear a lot about plants, animals, and hiking. Whether you take day hikes or go backpacking, you'll enjoy this park more if you know the special meaning of these Shenandoah words.

backpack	to hike with gear strapped to your back, and to camp in backcountry or wilderness
backpacker stove	small, lightweight stove; the only manmade fire allowed in backcountry—See page 41.
basking rock	place where snakes lie in sun
bearproof	to hang food at least ten feet above ground some distance from campsite; also to keep food smells off yourself, tent, and sleeping bag—The Park Service bearproofs trash cans and signs. See page 35.
blaze	mark on tree or rock that guides hikers along a trail—Each color means something. *white*—Appalachian Trail; no horses *blue*—Shenandoah foot trail *yellow*—horse trail with foot travel allowed
bushwhacker	hiker that goes off trails with map and compass, deep into woods and thickets
cavity nesters	animals that make their homes in holes in trees
circuit hike	one that goes in a loop so hiker need not retrace steps
compass	instrument with magnetic needle that points to magnetic north and helps you find your direction

day hike	one that doesn't include an overnight stay in the backcountry
erosion	wearing or cutting away of earth and rock by the action of wind and water or hikers' feet
exposure	see *hypothermia*
hibernacula	place where animals hibernate
hollow	small valley or basin
hypothermia	illness caused by a drop in body temperature, also called exposure; can cause death
impact	force against
lava	hot melted rock (magma) that flows from a volcano or a crack in the earth's crust
lightning	electricity jumping from clouds to ground—Avoid by getting off peaks and ridges and staying away from lone rocks or trees. Note, a person on a horse acts as a "lightning rod," or target to catch electricity
liners	lightweight socks worn inside heavy wool socks with hiking boots
litter	bad news—trash or garbage in the wrong place—If you can carry it into the country, you can carry it out.
low-impact camping	staying in the backcountry overnight without leaving any sign that you were there—Park rules say only two days in one backcountry campsite.
moleskin	heavy felt bandage used to prevent blisters
pack it out	carry it out of the wilderness
packs	*backpack*—large cloth sack with compartments, carried on a frame on your back along with bedroll *day pack*—cloth sack carried on back for day hikes
permit	free registration that allows hiker to camp overnight in backcountry
predator	animal that survives by killing and eating other animals
prey	animal caught and eaten by another animal
raptor	bird of prey, a predator
regulations	rules—Ask for a copy of park rules. One rule is, "Don't feed the animals."
run	creek or stream
snag	dead tree in which many animals often nest—See *cavity nesters*.
succession	order in which one kind of plant grows and crowds out another type—Different animals are attracted to different types of plants, so an *animal succession* follows a plant succession.
switchback	zigzag in a trail which makes a climb easier and prevents erosion
thicket	area with many shrubs close together
topo	topographic map; chart that shows great detail of land surfaces including hills, valleys, rivers, roads, and buildings
trace	what's left of an old road or trail
trail head	beginning of trail
uplift	rising of earth's crust
waffle stompers	boots with lug soles that look a bit like waffles; friends to hikers, foes to ferns
weathering	breaking up and wearing away of earth and rocks, caused by tree roots, chemical action, and temperature changes
weight	heaviness—Your pack should be no heavier than 1/5 of your own weight.

To Know a Mountain

Your family can travel the length of Skyline Drive in a car. Roadside mile markers and a purchased *Park Guide* show you where to stop and learn the Shenandoah story. But if you really want to *know* the mountains and all they have to offer, two feet are better than four wheels. Pick a trail or two and hike!

Most trails go down, so the second half of a hike is often the hardest part. If you hike down for 15 minutes, it may take 30 or 40 minutes to walk back up. With this is mind, and a day pack with canteen on your back, you're off on a mountain experience.

Notice the change in trees as you change elevation. What plants smile up at you from beside the trail? Does it get warmer or cooler as you go? What do the rocks tell you about this changing earth?

On your way uphill, rest stops will be a time for quiet thought. Imagine what it was like to live here before the settlers came. Think how it was to live in a log cabin down in a hollow. Listen to the mountain and its creatures. Smell the growing things. Feel the forever-ness of Shenandoah National Park.

Spring Hike

Wood Betony

Different Elevation—Different Trees

Earth Story 1

The Indians knew Shenandoah. One of their legends tells how these mountains were formed. At first there was no earth, just a huge body of water, and all creatures lived in the sky. When the sky became too crowded, they sent a water beetle down to look for land. The beetle dove to the bottom of the sea and came up with a bit of mud. The mud grew and grew until it was as big as the world, but it was too soft and wet.

The grandfather of all vultures was sent down to dry out the land with the beating of his wings. When the vulture got tired, he flew lower and lower. His wings dragged along through the mud and formed ridges, mountains, and valleys.

The Indians called the earth their mother. They tried to show respect and care for her. Of her they sang, "Before me peaceful, behind me peaceful, under me peaceful, over me peaceful. All around me peaceful. Peaceful voice when it speaks. The earth is everlasting and peaceful. I am at peace with the earth."

"I Am At Peace With The Earth" ▶

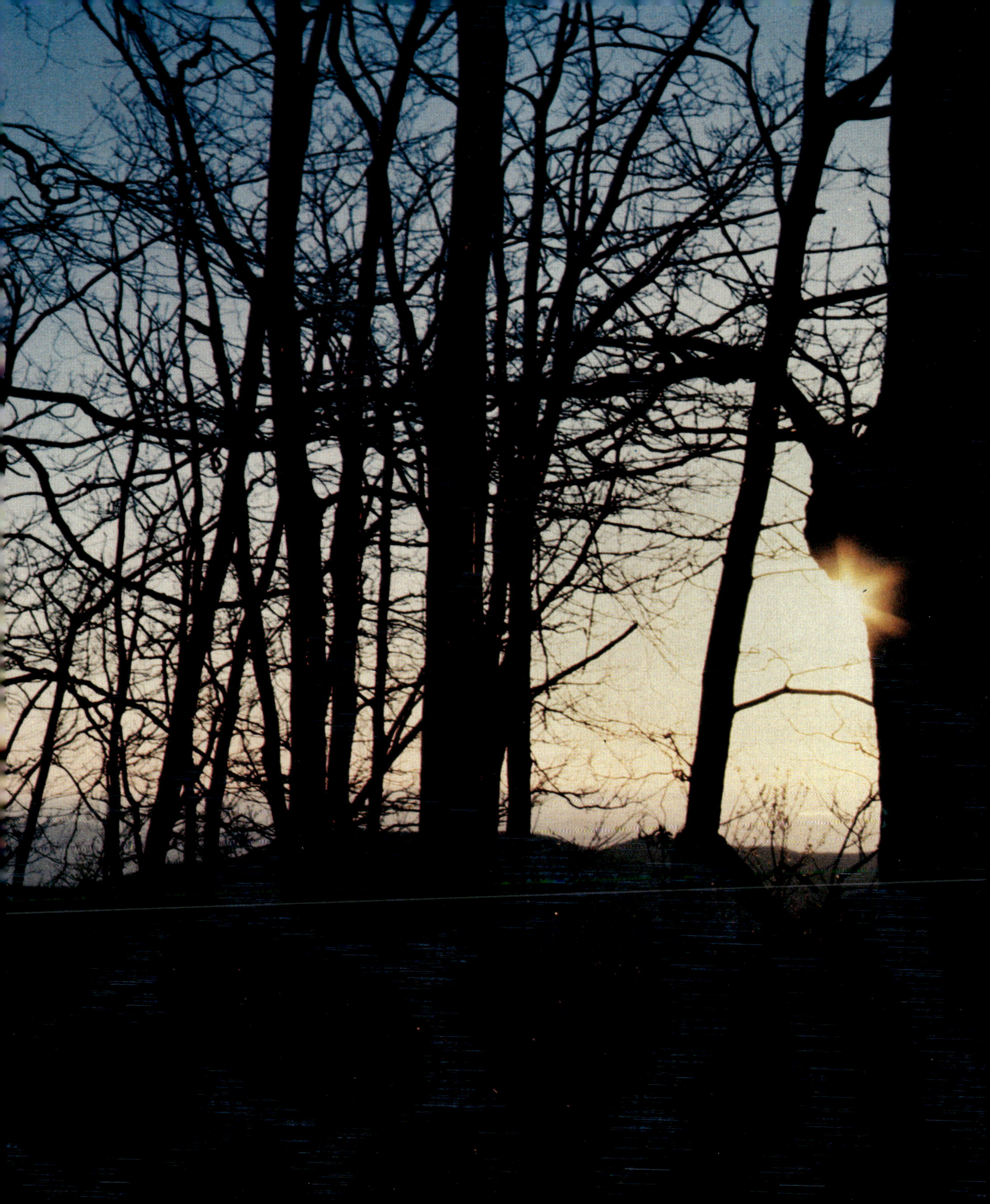

Earth Story II

Scientists tell a less peaceful tale. They say the "basement rocks" were formed 1100 million years ago. Those rocks were slowly lifted by earth forces until they formed very high mountains.

Even as the mountains rose, they were being worn down by erosion. When the rocks cracked, lava flowed to the surface and buried the mountains. As this lava-covered plain cooled, it cracked the way drying mud cracks. The cracks extended down several feet and formed columns of lava, or basalt.

Later the plain sank and was covered by a shallow sea. Sand and mud washed into the sea and fell to the bottom, forming layers of sediment.

After millions of years, the earth began to rise and the sea drained away. The rising earth folded itself into a mountain range now called the Appalachians. Erosion has smoothed the mountains into rounded ridges. Shenandoah straddles one of them, the Blue Ridge Mountains of Virginia. Now you can see where erosion has uncovered basement rocks, basalt columns, and other rocks that tell the story of this changing earth.

Old Rag Mountain

Basalt Columns Metamorphosed Into Greenstone

450 Million-Year-Old Greenstone

Plant Parade —Succession

Plants now cover many of those ancient rocks in Shenandoah National Park. But plants also changed throughout millions of years. First came the "pioneer plants," lichens and mosses. As they grew, they made an acid that ate into the rocks. Bits and pieces broke off the rocks and mixed with dead and decaying plants. Over thousands of years, these bits of rock and dead plant material built up a soil rich enough to support ferns, grasses, shrubs, and finally trees.

This parade of changing plants is called *plant succession.* Many different plant successions have taken place in these mountains since the first person walked among the trees. And as you walk through the forest, you'll see this endless cycle beginning again. Lichens, ferns, and mosses grow on rocks and tree trunks. Mushrooms and other fungi spring up among rotting roots of dead trees. The rocks and trees break down and become soil where seeds sprout and grow.

Out of death, life begins anew.

Fern

Part of Plant Succession—Cinnamon Fern

Shelf Fungus On Dead Bark

Morel Mushroom

Flowers

In spring, Shenandoah is a wild flower show. Bloodroot flowers burst, starlike, through late snow. Their green leaves grow larger after their blossoms fade. Trillium comes along in May and changes from white to pink. White, yellow, and violet flowers all sprout in the wet soil warmed by the spring sun's rays.

Who gifted the forest with such riches? How were these seeds planted and why? What is the grand design?

A flower's powdery pollen is carried by wind and insects to another flower. This brings the male sperms of one blossom to the female ova of another flower of the same kind. Sperms and ova combine and make the lower part of the bloom swell into a fruit or seed pod. When the pods break open, seeds scatter. Some are eaten by birds and mice, pass through the animals, and fall to the ground. Prickly or sticky seeds may hitch rides on fur or feathers and land in soil. They stay there until the next spring's rain and sun make them sprout.

What would happen if you and a million other visitors picked the wild flowers this year?

Azalea

Bloodroot

Jack-In-The-Pulpit

Common Blue Violets

Common Trillium

Rue Anemone

Trees

And who plants the trees? The local squirrels bury acorns and hickory nuts to eat when winter comes. Some nuts and acorns stay buried and have a chance to sprout. Other trees grow from root systems of "parent trees."

There are more than 100 types of trees at Shenandoah. Most of them are deciduous trees with wide leaves that fall every autumn. Ash, elm, hickory, maple, oak: you'll find these and more.

Other trees stay green all year, so we call them evergreens. Some have wide leaves, but most have needles and cones. Evergreens with cones are called conifers. Eastern hemlock, balsam fir, white pine, red spruce, and pitch pine are some of the evergreens at Shenandoah.

With so many trees to enjoy, you may wonder how you can tell one from the other. You could learn the shape of each kind. Or you can look at its flower, bark, leaves, or needles. Yellow birch bark looks as if thin paper is peeling off the trunk. Maple and oak leaves are easy to recognize by their shapes. Hemlock needles are short, flat, and shiny. Pitch pine needles grow in bunches of three.

Trees Pry Rocks Apart

Pine Cone

Hemlock

Yellow Birch

Dogwood Blooms

Redbud Tree

And More Trees

But trees are more than bark, leaves, and needles, more than toothpicks and two-by-four lumber.

Trees make soil. Their roots pry rocks apart. Then erosion and weathering reduce the rocks to sand. Dead leaves and rotted stumps crumble and combine with the sand to make rich soil. Roots of living trees hold soil and keep it from washing away. And that soil holds water.

Trees provide leaves to line a chipmunk's nest—cones with seeds the red squirrel eats—twigs for deer to browse—holes where chickadees nest—and branches where owls perch to give a hoot.

Green leaves take carbon dioxide, the gas given off by breathing animals, and convert it back into oxygen for the air we breathe. Recycled air? Yes, the air you need for life.

Take time to sit under an oak tree and ponder. Feel its rough bark. Smell its fallen leaves becoming part of the soil. Look up into its armlike branches that may someday shade your great-great-grandchildren. It *could* live that long, you know, because it's protected in Shenandoah National Park.

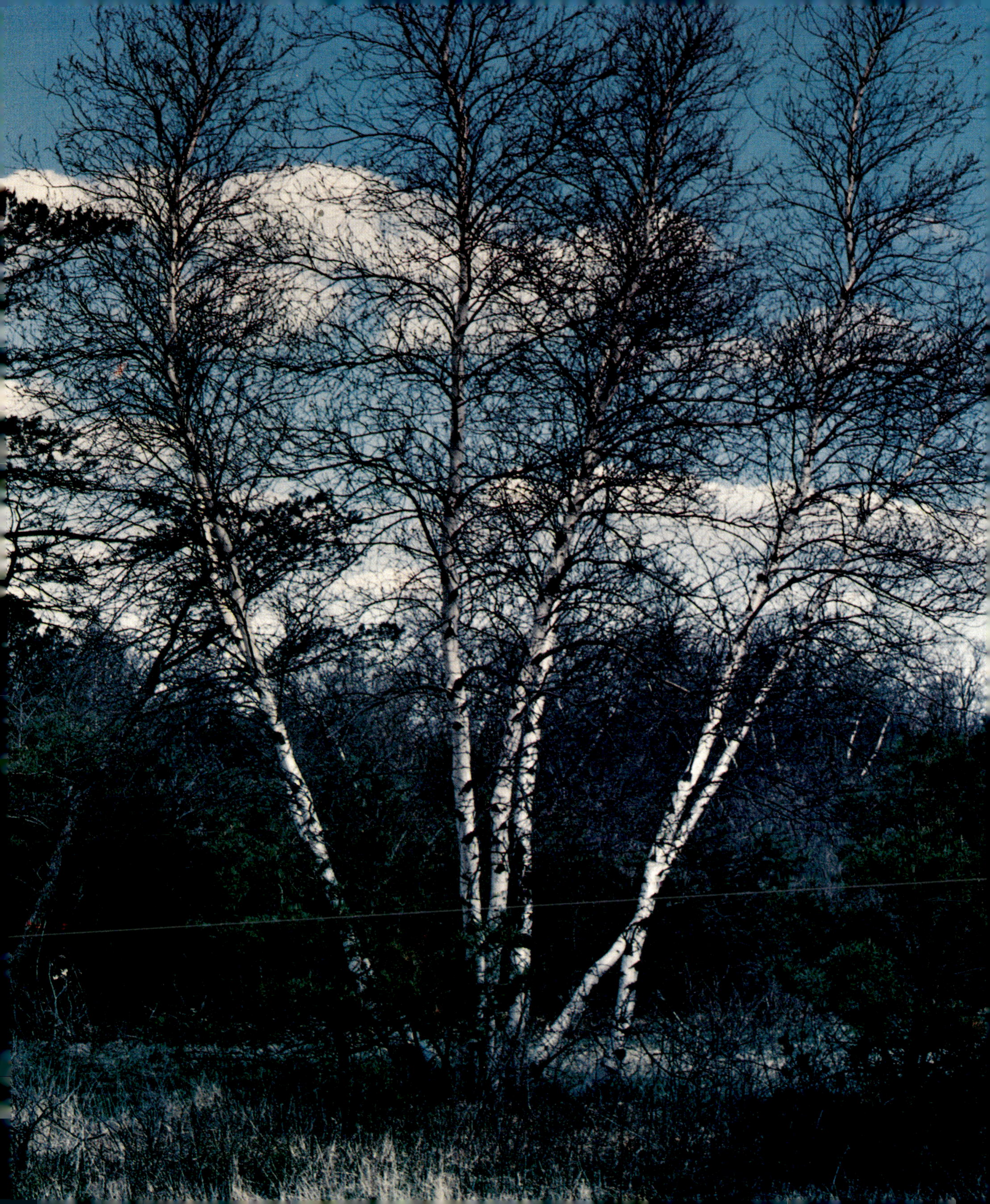

Early Days

Thousands of years ago, Indians who camped here may have thanked the Great Spirit who made trees. They made spoons from elm, poplar, and sycamore. They carved bows out of black locust and arrows from hickory. Bark fibers were good for bowstrings, fish nets, and animal traps.

Early in the 1700s, settlers from Europe came and pushed the Indians off the land they had cleared in the valley. As more people came, all the flat land was soon taken. Latecomers made homes higher in the hollows and up on ridges.

These mountain farmers planted corn and apples and kept pigs and cows. They chopped the bark around trees to deaden them so the sun could reach their crops.

They did well for awhile, farming and bartering, or trading with each other. They managed to live off the land until the richness of the soil was used up. Crops became poor, and people needed money to buy what they could no longer produce. They sold chestnut and chestnut oak bark for leather tanning to people in the valley. They pulled logs down the mountain to sell. Life was hard for the mountain people.

Cabins Sag

Chimneys Crumble

Where Kettles Boiled, Waffles Baked

This Was A Stove—

"Recycled" Park

Late in the 1800s, George Freeman Pollock developed a vacation resort in the Blue Ridge Mountains. Visitors came to this resort called Skyland to rest and enjoy outdoor living.

When the U.S. government planned to set aside some eastern national parks, friends urged Mr. Pollock to work toward having the crest of the Blue Ridge included in a park. He and other people worked hard, but park land had to be bought and given free to the federal government. Half the money to buy the land for Shenandoah National Park came from ordinary people's pockets and purses. The other half was given by the government of the state of Virginia.

Some farmers didn't want to sell their land and other residents had no place to go. But finally, when all the problems were solved, President Franklin Roosevelt arrived to dedicate this park on July 3, 1936. Skyline Drive was completed in 1939.

The mountain folks' homes were taken down. Fields and pastures were left to nature, and a new plant succession began. Shenandoah became the nation's first "recycled" park.

Virginia's Gift To You ▶

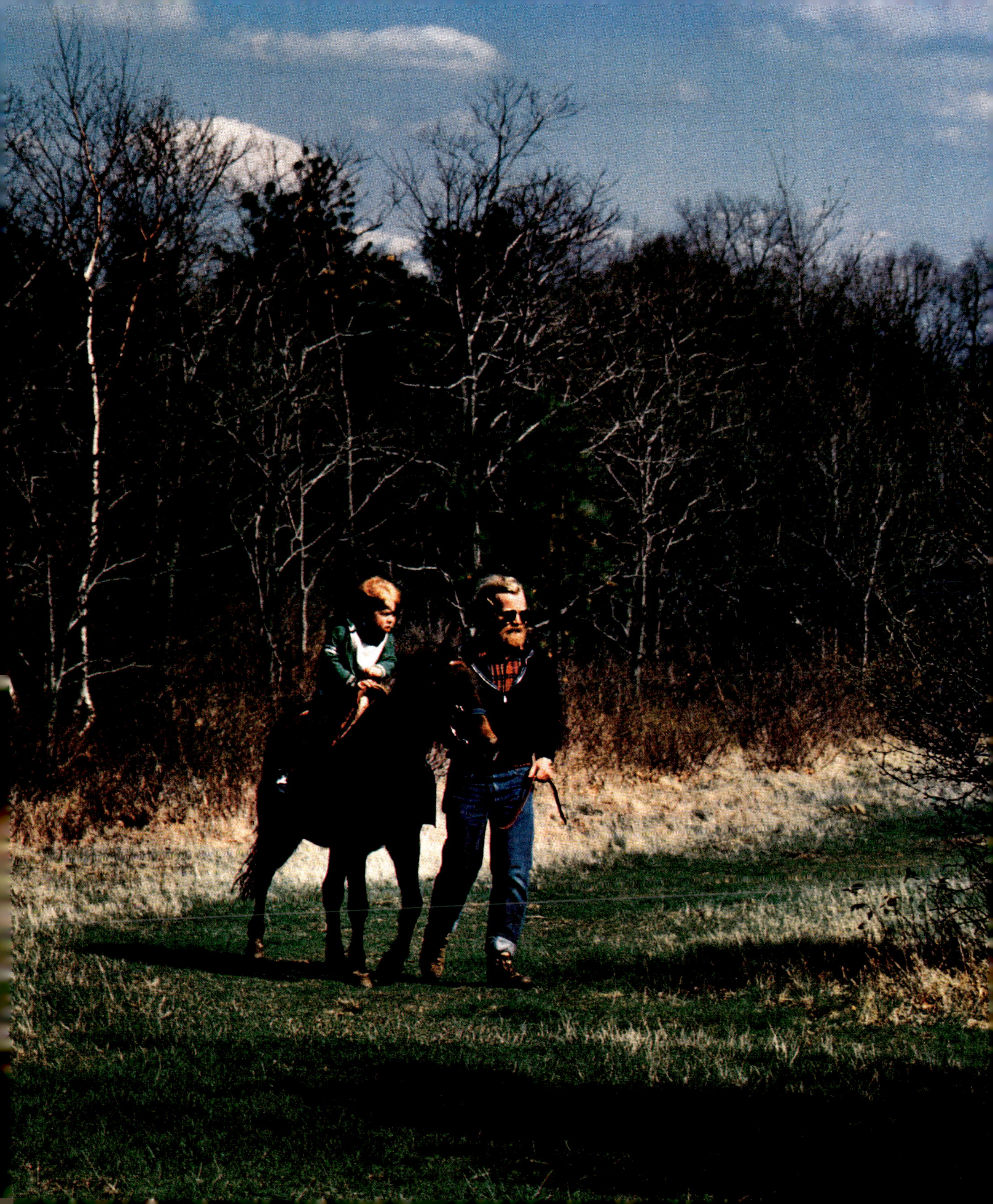

Plan to be Safe

Every national park has its dangers, and perhaps the main one is being in a new, unfamiliar place. Visitors may not realize they need to look before they step and see before they reach.

Warm rock walls or paved walkways are cozy places where snakes can snuggle during the cool of night. But a flashlight will help a person see any snakes and avoid them.

The rocks at the top and sides of a waterfall are covered with slippery moss. These are poor places to explore. Besides, you can enjoy a waterfall's awesome beauty and take better pictures from an observation point. Trail markers usually lead you to the best places where walls and railings often remind you to take care of yourself.

What seems like a perfect, warm hiking day can turn into a cold, wet one. If you are prepared, a stormy day can still be a hiking day with no danger of "exposure," or hypothermia, which could end your stay on this earth.

Maps, good gear, and careful planning will give you a happy, safe stay at Shenandoah National Park.

South River Falls

Timber Rattler

Poison Ivy

Furry Friends

Furry animals can be another danger. Most people know enough to keep away from bears. But deer can also be dangerous. To protect themselves or their young, deer will rear up on their hind legs and lash out with sharp front hoofs.

Chipmunks, ground squirrels, and woodchucks look like cuddly stuffed animals. But park people hope you will leave them to "stuff" themselves on grasses, seeds, and flowering plants. If you feed them bread or peanuts, you could be scratched or bitten. Then you'd need a tetanus shot or several shots to prevent rabies. These animals may also carry plague, which can be carried from animals to humans by fleas.

Aside from the danger to you, there is a danger to animals when you feed them. They need to eat their own natural foods in order to make the kind of body fat they need to get through the winter. If you feed them, they won't gather acorns and seeds to store in their burrows. The best way to enjoy furry friends is to sit quietly and be patient. When you become part of the scenery, they may allow you to watch them in their forest home.

Furry Friend—Eastern Cottontail Rabbit

Chipmunk

Woodchuck

Deer, Oh Deer

You may or may not be lucky enough to see wildlife at Shenandoah National Park. But one thing is certain: the wildlife will see you.

Hundreds of different bird songs trill from the trees. But search as you may, most of the singers escape from your view. Do their eyes look at you?

Early and late in the day, you will see whitetail deer along Skyline Drive. When you approach, they bound off, showing their flared white tails. Later, their black, shiny eyes look out at you from behind the trees.

A mother deer, or doe, has only one fawn the first time she has young. After that she usually has two fawns every spring.

Fawns are protected by spots on their backs that make them blend into the shrubs. They have no smell, or scent, so their mother leaves them in a bushy thicket and browses nearby. Her scent could attract a predator, so she stays away from her fawns except when she goes to nurse them.

In four days the fawns follow their mother. They learn the ways of the deer until the next year when their mother mates again to have more young.

Female Deer, Or Doe

Fawn

Bear Country

Many wild creatures disappeared from these mountains before they were protected by a national park. In 1935, a few deer were released here. Now there are more than a thousand.

The black bear came back by itself. Will you see one? Let's hope you don't see a bear nose to nose. To avoid this, you can bearproof your campsite. Hang food at least ten feet up between two trees or keep it locked in a car trunk away from your sleeping place. Be sure that you, your bedroll, and tent do not smell of food or sweet-scented lotion. Don't even have chewing gum with you.

Bears spend most of their time hunting for food. Do them a favor and make sure they don't find your food. They need to eat what the land provides: berries, apples, ants, roots, and sometimes squirrels and mice.

And try not to get between a mother bear and her cubs. Your eyesight is probably better than a bear's. But a bear's hearing and sense of smell are better than yours. You can keep from surprising a bear by careful watching and by making noise as you walk the trail. Sing, talk, whistle, or hang a bell on your pack.

Black Bear

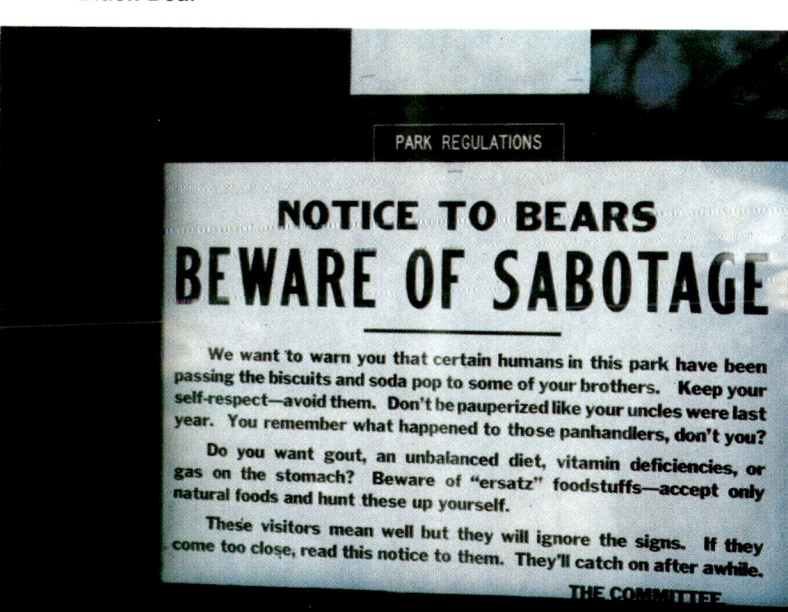

NOTICE TO BEARS
BEWARE OF SABOTAGE

We want to warn you that certain humans in this park have been passing the biscuits and soda pop to some of your brothers. Keep your self-respect—avoid them. Don't be pauperized like your uncles were last year. You remember what happened to those panhandlers, don't you?

Do you want gout, an unbalanced diet, vitamin deficiencies, or gas on the stomach? Beware of "ersatz" foodstuffs—accept only natural foods and hunt these up yourself.

These visitors mean well but they will ignore the signs. If they come too close, read this notice to them. They'll catch on after awhile.

THE COMMITTEE

Notice To Bears

Bearproofed Sign

Big Meadow

Be sure to explore that huge, open space at mile 51, Big Meadow. You'll see the way much of this area looked when it was still farmland. At that time the crest of the Blue Ridge had many manmade meadows.

Most likely, such meadows were created by Indians and later maintained by farmers. To keep this last meadow open, the National Park Service used to mow it. Now they use fire control. After a burn, pioneer plants grow: ferns, fireweed, grasses, and pine seedlings. Left alone without burning, these plants would give way to a forest succession. It would become an oak forest like most of the Blue Ridge. Wildlife would change, too.

Big Meadow is a "museum" where you can see plant succession, a deer "nursery," birds, and other animals.

Spring brings the woodchucks out from their winter dens. Tall grass and flowers promise protection and food. The does hide their fawns in hawthorn thickets. Birds of many kinds come here to feed. Don't miss your "meadow museum."

Meadow's Edge

Burnet

Rufous-Sided Towhee

A Guide to Forever?

Go with a park ranger on a guided hike as soon as you can. This will help you "tune-in" to the world of plants and animals. The ranger may ask you to get down and try a mouse-eye view of the meadow. Look around and see which plants you might eat and what you'd use to pad your mouse nest. Or will you be a smooth green snake and thread your way, unseen, through tall grass looking for a tasty spider?

Another guided hike may take you to the top of Black Rock. There you'll stand on million-year-old rocks and look way out into "forever."

On Limberlost Trail, you'll see an old stand of hemlocks. This is one of the few stands of trees untouched by the lumberman's ax. But it's OK for you to touch the shiny green needles of these big old evergreens.

Along the meadow's edge, an early morning birdwalk will be a time to hear a warbler's tune. Blue jays and towhees will fly by, and a drum sound may tell you a ruffed grouse is courting his mate.

After one or two guided hikes, trees, flowers, and rocks will mean more to you. The wilderness will become a part of your life.

Guided Meadow Hike

"Into Forever?"

Wilderness Ways

What is a wilderness? It's a place where roads are not allowed to chop the landscape into plots and blocks. People who go there are guests beside a mountain stream, in a bear's hollow, or a good distance from a snake's basking rock.

But as more and more hikers set out on the trails, the wilderness gets less wild. Does it seem like a wilderness when you find gum wrappers, soda cans, and broken glass at a campsite? How do you feel when you see bright orange or red tents dotting a mountainside? Do you want to hear loud music or the wind rushing through red maple leaves?

People who love the backcountry pack out all of their trash. And truly devoted bushwhackers even pack out litter left by thoughtless hikers who haven't learned wilderness ways. They also leave pets and transistor radios at home and buy green or tan equipment that blends with the woods. Friends of the forest stay on trails and don't cut across switchbacks designed to prevent erosion and to make hiking easier.

Ask for and read a copy of park regulations when you register for a free backcountry use permit. And have a wonderful wilderness experience!

Know Your Wilderness Ways

Backpacker Stove

Winter

While you're hiking up and down the trails, enjoying jack-in-the-pulpits and avoiding poison ivy, others have serious work to do. Ants and beavers spend all summer storing food in their homes. The woodchuck must eat all the time, getting fat enough to hibernate until spring.

When days grow short, insect-eating birds fly south, but seed-eaters and those that eat insect eggs and larvae stay on. In winter they save their energy and don't do much singing. Even leaves must make food so the trees can store it in trunks and roots in order to live through the winter.

Winter scenes may be covered in white. But snow melts now and then, leaving the trees gaunt and gray. Sometimes trees and shrubs are coated with ice from frozen fog or rain. If the ice gets too thick on the trees, winter silence is broken by the cracking and crashing of branches.

Shenandoah is usually open in winter. And this is when a few fearless travelers come to enjoy a quiet park where they are almost alone.

Winter

Big Meadows In Winter

Ice Storms Leave Ice Art

A Changing World

The only thing that stays the same in Shenandoah is the fact that these northern Blue Ridge Mountains are forever changing. On the trail to Stony Man, you see those trees, working away, changing the rocks. During your walk, even the sky may change from blue to gray. Or still, windless air will change from warm and damp to cool and breezy.

How will you and other visitors change Shenandoah? Will you add to erosion by cutting across a switchback? Or will you remind a friend to leave the wild flowers to make their seeds?

What change will Shenandoah bring into your life? Hiking will make your legs stronger. Your vision will be sharper from watching for wildlife. You may get to know more trees, flowers, and animals. What memories will you take home so you can "replay" your park experience some Tuesday after school?

Let's hope you feel thankful that Virginians and others wanted to set aside a mountain ridge for the rest of the world to enjoy. They must have known you'd need a wilderness where you can sing, "I'm at peace with the world."

How Will It Change? ▶

Other National Park Service Areas in the East

The BLUE RIDGE PARKWAY connects Shenandoah National Park with the North Carolina side of Great Smoky Mountains National Park. This is not a high-speed road, but a scenic drive bordered by white pines and colorful azaleas and rhododendrons. Farmhouses and barns surrounded by green fields make picture postcard scenes for you to enjoy.

Campgrounds, picnic areas, and trails makes you want to stop and stay in this National Park area.

GREAT SMOKY MOUNTAINS NATIONAL PARK, on the border between North Carolina and Tennessee, was created by an act of Congress at the same time as Shenandoah National Park. History comes alive when you visit an old farm at Oconaluftee on the North Carolina side. In Tennessee you might sit at a desk in the Greenbrier School or visit some farms in Cades Cove. Spring flowers, fall colors, and the Appalachian Trail draw millions of visitors every year to Great Smoky.

Most of ACADIA NATIONAL PARK is on Mount Desert Island off the coast of Maine. This pink granite island offers mountain hikes and tide pool walks. On a guided geology hike, a naturalist explains how glaciers grooved and polished the granite and how fjords were formed.

Indian artifacts in a museum tell some of the Indian history of this island. Boat trips to Baker and Little Cranberry Islands give a view of French, English, and colonial times in America.

Acadia National Park and EVERGLADES NATIONAL PARK are very different from one another and totally distinct from Shenandoah and Great Smoky. You'll enjoy Acadia in summer. Everglades is a good place to be in winter. The Everglades is a flat "sea" of sawgrass, dotted with cypress heads (clumps) and hammocks made of hardwood trees.

This park is a paradise for plant lovers, birdwatchers, and reptile fanciers. Be sure to take some old pants and tennis shoes you can throw away after you go with a naturalist on a swamp tromp or slough slog. It's a wet or muddy adventure you won't want to miss.

Author and Illustrators

Writing books about the national parks has taken Wyoming-born Ruth Radlauer from the gentle mountains and hollows of Shenandoah National Park to the granite peaks of Yosemite. From Maine to Hawaii, Alaska to the Virgin Islands, she has discovered the natural treasures of the United States as preserved in its national parks.

Graduates of the University of California at Los Angeles, Ed and Ruth Radlauer are authors of over 200 books for young people. Along with their adult daughter and sons, they photograph and write about a wide variety of subjects, ranging from dolls to drag racing and monkeys to minibikes.

* * * *

Ruth and Ed are grateful to all the personnel of 20 national parks, who have helped in countless ways to create this series, PARKS FOR PEOPLE.